DREAMLAND

Learn with
PHONICS

SHORT VOWEL SOUNDS

BOOK 2

Author
Lata Seth

Published by

DREAMLAND PUBLICATIONS
J-128, KIRTI NAGAR, NEW DELHI - 110 015 (INDIA)
Ph. : 011-2543 5657, 2510 6050 Fax. : 011-2543 8283
E-mail : dreamland@vsnl.com
www.dreamlandpublications.com

Published in 2014 by
DREAMLAND PUBLICATIONS
J-128, Kirti Nagar, New Delhi - 110 015 (India)
Tel : 011-2510 6050, Fax : 011-2543 8283
E-mail : dreamland@vsnl.com, www.dreamlandpublications.com
ISBN : 978-93-5089-531-3
Printed by
Haploos Printing House

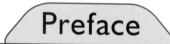

Preface

Phonics is a method of teaching how to read using the sounds that letters represent. This series is a set of 5 books beginning with sounds connected with 26 letters of the English alphabet, short and long vowels and progressing to letter blends. The series has been especially designed for young learners aged 3 to 7 to help them become good readers. Words represented with pictures enhance and encourage independent learning and strengthen the spelling skills. A variety of exercises and engaging activities offer essential practice and inspire young learners to test what they have learnt. These workbook-based phonics books are recommended for young learners as well as teachers and parents who want to teach their children the art of reading.

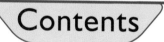

Contents

Order of Lessons

Introduction

1
-ad
-ag
-am

2
-an
-ap
-at

3
-ed
-eg
-en
-et

4
-ib
-id
-ig
-in

Let Us Revise 1 (Chapters 1-4)

5

-ip   -it   -ix

6

-og   -op   -ot   -ox

7

-ub   -ug   -up

8

-ud   -un   -ut

Let Us Revise 2 (Chapters 5-8)
Let Us Review.

Introduction

Hi! what are we going to learn in this book?

Well, in Book 1 we read about single-letter sounds. As we all know, the letters *a, e, i, o, u* are vowels. They have two sounds each: *short sound* and *long sound*. In this book, we will learn the *short vowel sounds*. When only one vowel is used in a word, it makes a short sound. Children will be taught the short vowel sounds using different *word families*.

Word families are groups of words having a common pattern. They consist of the same combinations of letters in them and a similar sound. For example, *sad*, *dad*, and *bad* are a family of words with the 'ad' sound and common letter combination.

Come, read these vowels with me.

A   E   I   O   U

1

-ad -ag -am

In this chapter, we will use word families with -ad, -ag and -am sounds of short vowel a.

Read loudly and listen to the short sound of vowel a.

d + ad = dad   b + ag = bag   j + am = jam

Here are some more new words for you.

-ad

lad   sad   pad   bad

-ag

wag   tag   rag   nag

-am

yam   dam   ram   mam

Time to Solve

Say the names of the pictures and fill in
the missing letters.

b _ _

d _ _

r _ _

s _ _

j _ _

r _ _

Look at the pictures and circle
their correct names.

mam dam

tag bag

rag wag

sad lad

mam yam

dad bad

7

Say the names of the pictures and match them to the correct words.

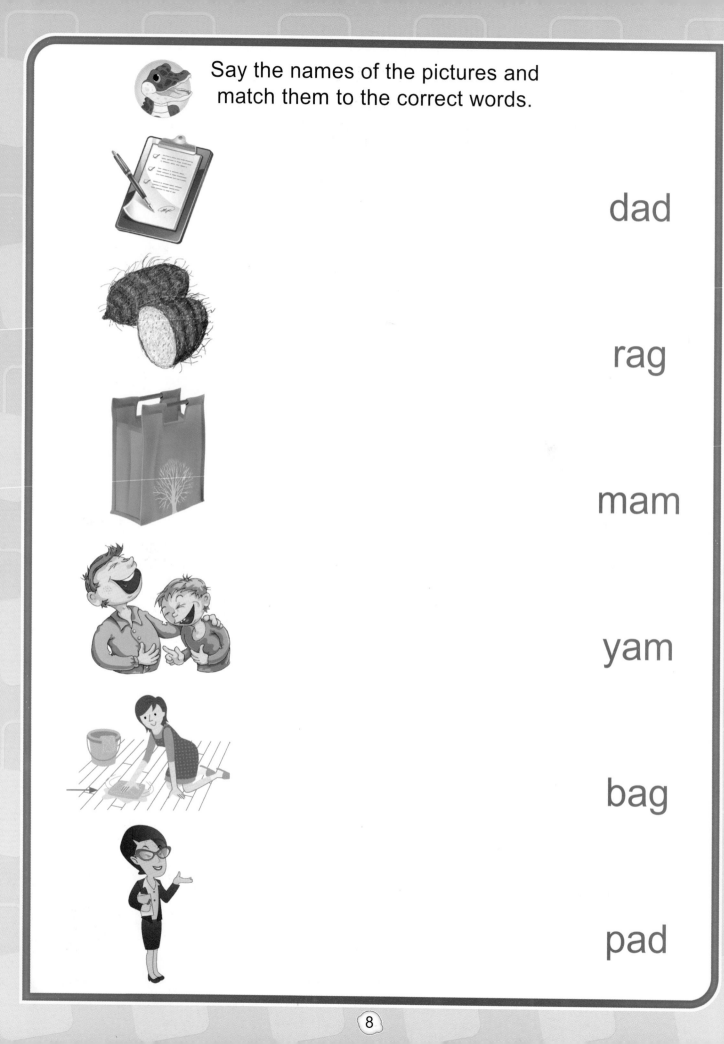

dad

rag

mam

yam

bag

pad

Say the names of the pictures and cross the one with sound not matching with its group.

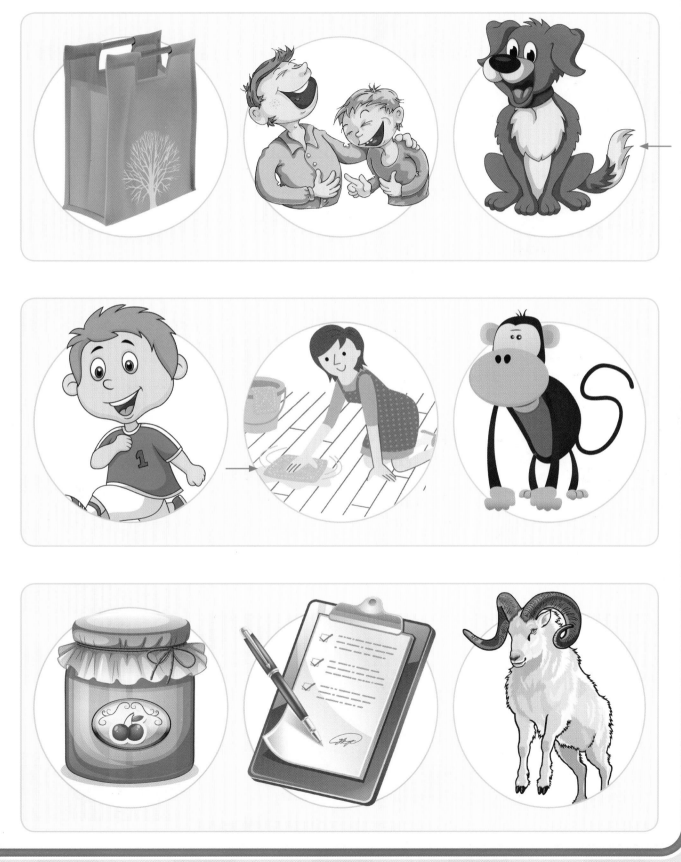

Unscramble the letters to get the correct names of the pictures.

add ------   amm------   arg ------

lda ------   mar ------   atg ------

Read the word and circle the correct picture.

mam

wag

pad

Fill each basket with the same sounding word.

dad

bag

jam

- -

Find the words in the box and write them.
Look at the pictures for clues.

| h | a | r | a | m | p |

- - - - - - - - - - - - - - - - - - -

| w | a | g | b | v | t |

- - - - - - - - - - - - - - - - - - -

| r | f | r | b | a | g |

- - - - - - - - - - - - - - - - - - -

Time to Chant

I and Sam love the yam,

Dad will come, and bring some jam;

We shall eat, yam with jam,

And shall go, to the dam, with the ram.

Story Time

Read this story aloud.

Sight Words — is, the

Paul is a sad lad.

His dog is bad.

The bad dog ate
the lad's jam.

Dad says, "Bad dog!".

Do at Home

Circle the -ad, -ag and -am words and also write them.
One has been done for you.

A (sad) lad with dad.

----

sad

A ram with yam at a dam.

A bag with a tag.

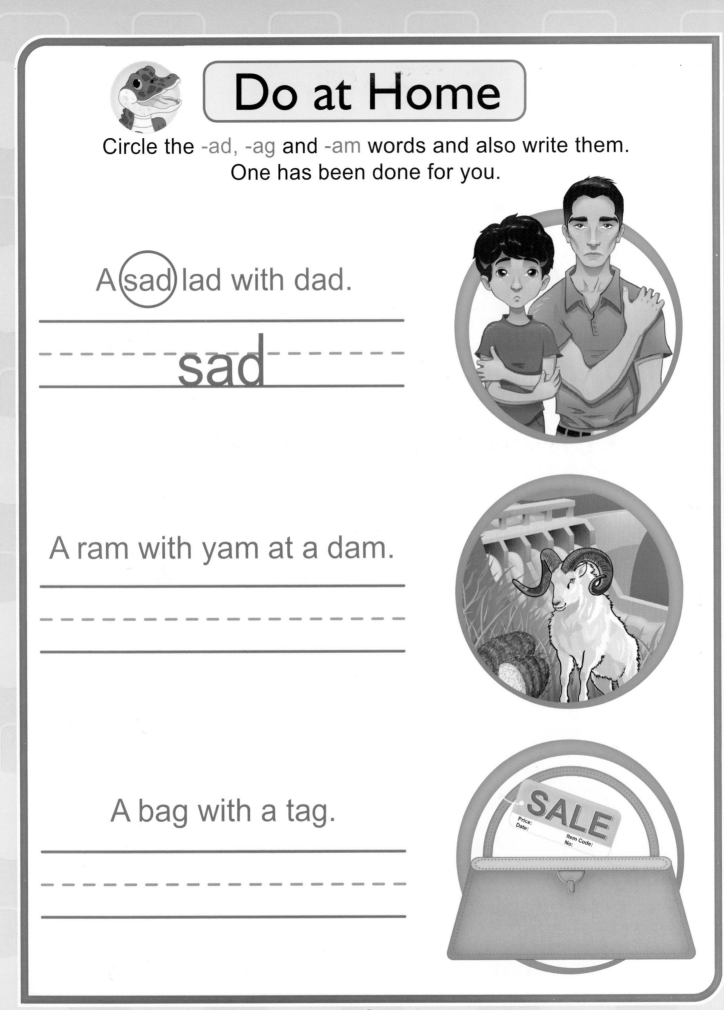

-an -ap -at

In this chapter, we will use word families with -an, -ap and -at sounds of short vowel a.

Read loudly and listen to the sound of short vowel a.

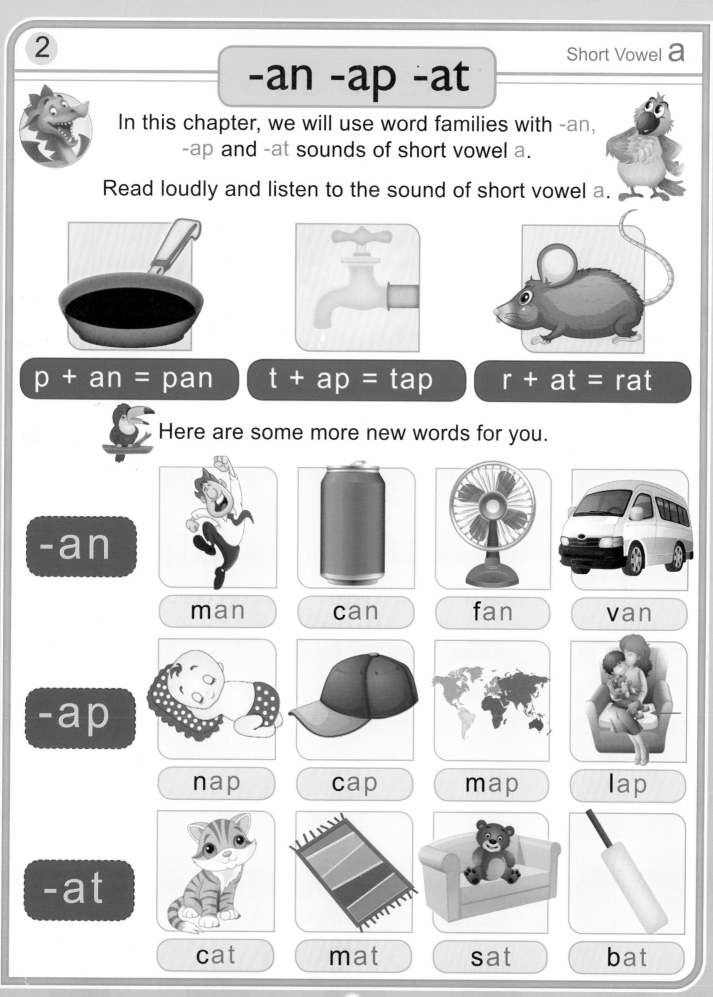

p + an = pan

t + ap = tap

r + at = rat

Here are some more new words for you.

-an

man

can

fan

van

-ap

nap

cap

map

lap

-at

cat

mat

sat

bat

Time to Solve

Unscramble the letters to get the correct names of the pictures.

anm ------- nap ------- ats -------

lpa ------- tar ------- atp -------

Read the word and circle the correct picture.

can

map

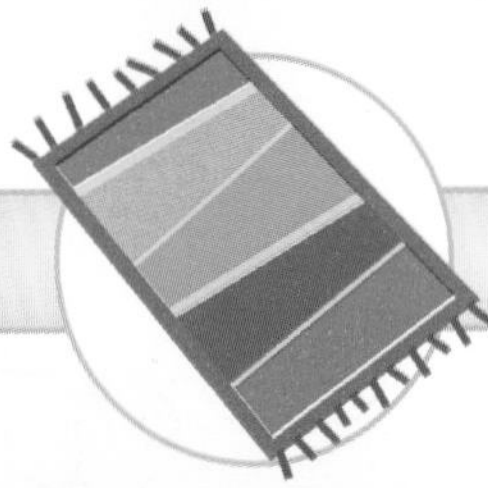

mat

Say the names of the pictures and fill in the missing letters.

c _ _   n _ _   r _ _

t _ _   s _ _   v _ _

 Look at the pictures and circle their correct names.

fan   man

tap   map

rat   cat

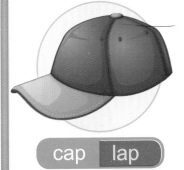

cap   lap

van   pan

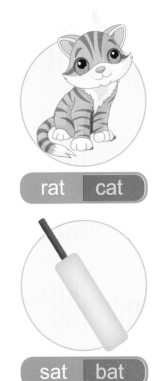

sat   bat

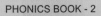

Say the names of the pictures and match them to the correct words.

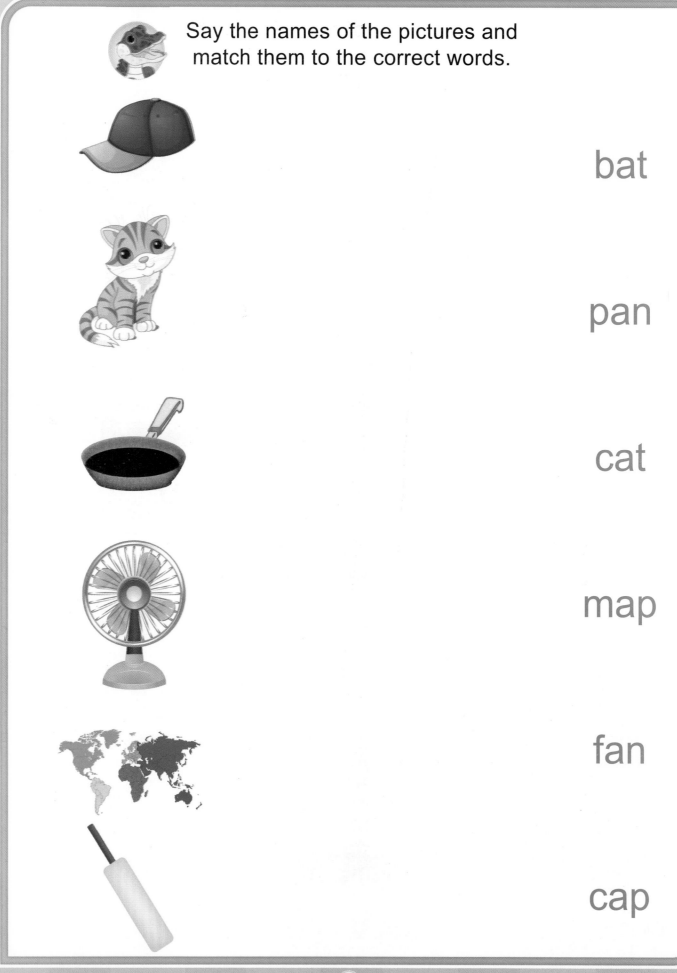

bat

pan

cat

map

fan

cap

Say the names of the pictures and cross the one with sound not matching with its group.

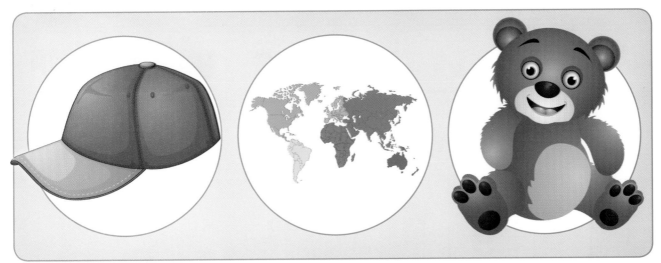

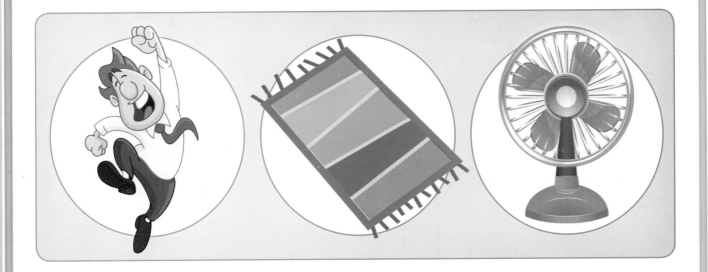

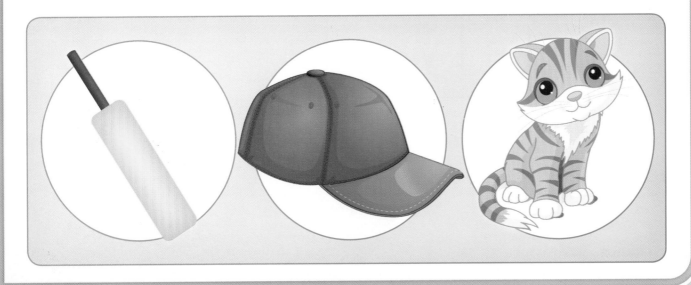

Find out the words given in the crossword.
You can look at the pictures for clues.

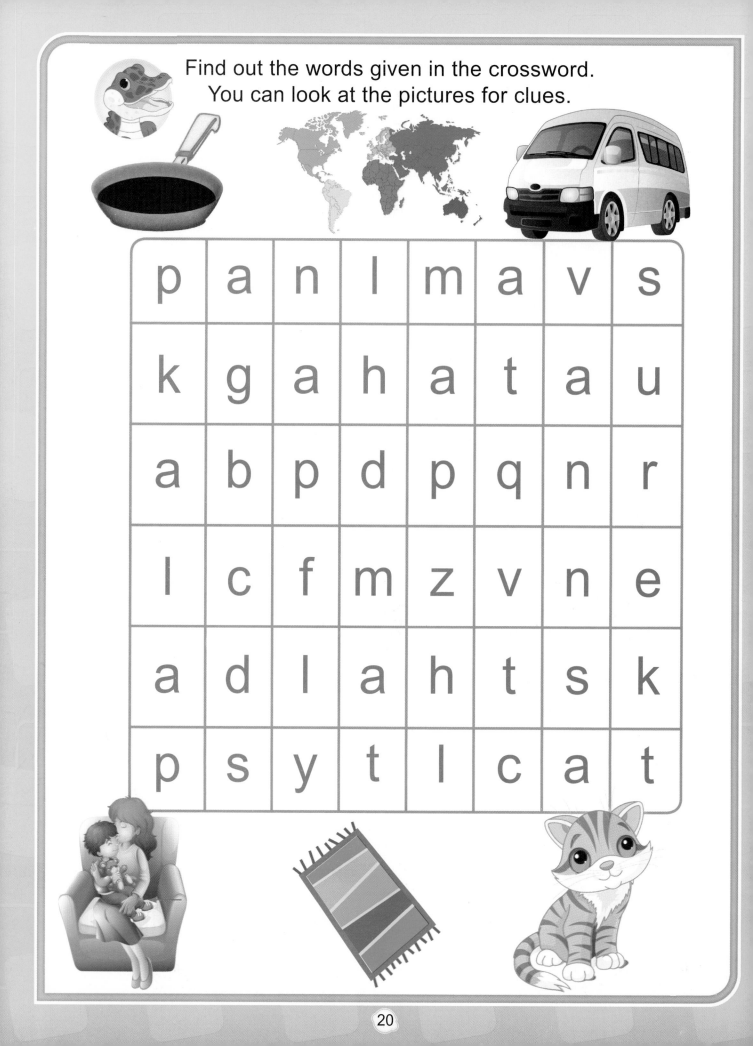

p	a	n	l	m	a	v	s
k	g	a	h	a	t	a	u
a	b	p	d	p	q	n	r
l	c	f	m	z	v	n	e
a	d	l	a	h	t	s	k
p	s	y	t	l	c	a	t

Time to Chant

A girl with a cap,

Looks at a map;

Her cat chases a rat,

The rat runs on a mat;

Wearing a cap.

Story Time

Read this story aloud.

Sight Words — a, with, in, the, on, at

A man with a pan.

A rat in the pan.

The cat jumps at the rat.

The pan falls on the mat.

Do at Home

Circle the -an, -ap and -at words and also write them. One has been done for you.

A (man) in a van.

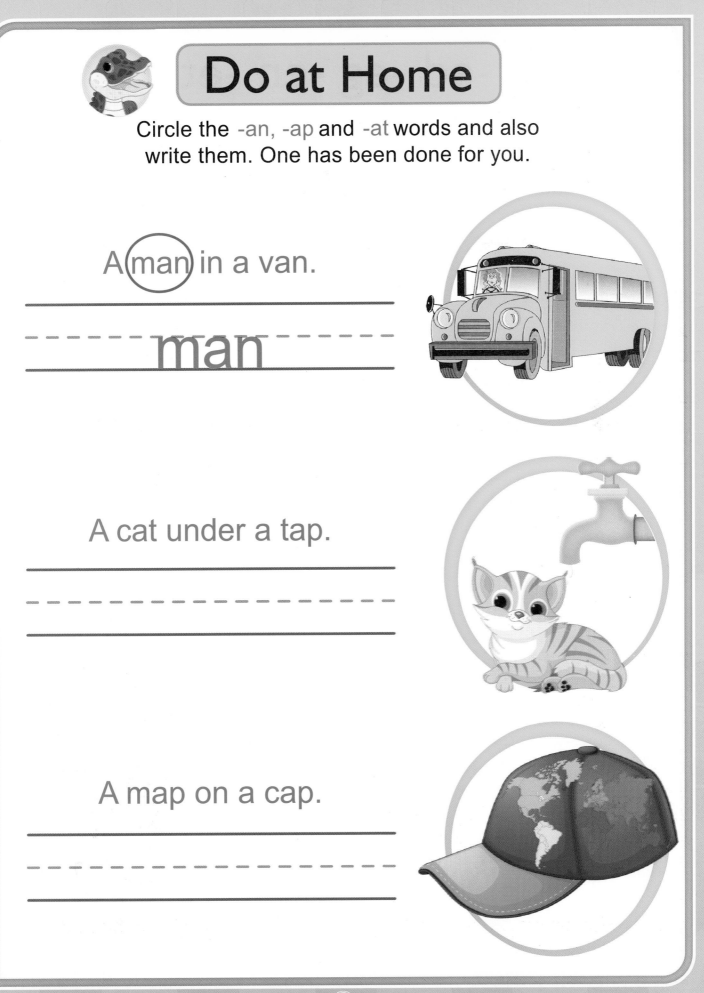

man

A cat under a tap.

A map on a cap.

-ed -eg -en -et

In this chapter, we will use word families with -ed, -eg, -en and -et sounds of short vowel e.

Read loudly and listen to the sound of short vowel e.

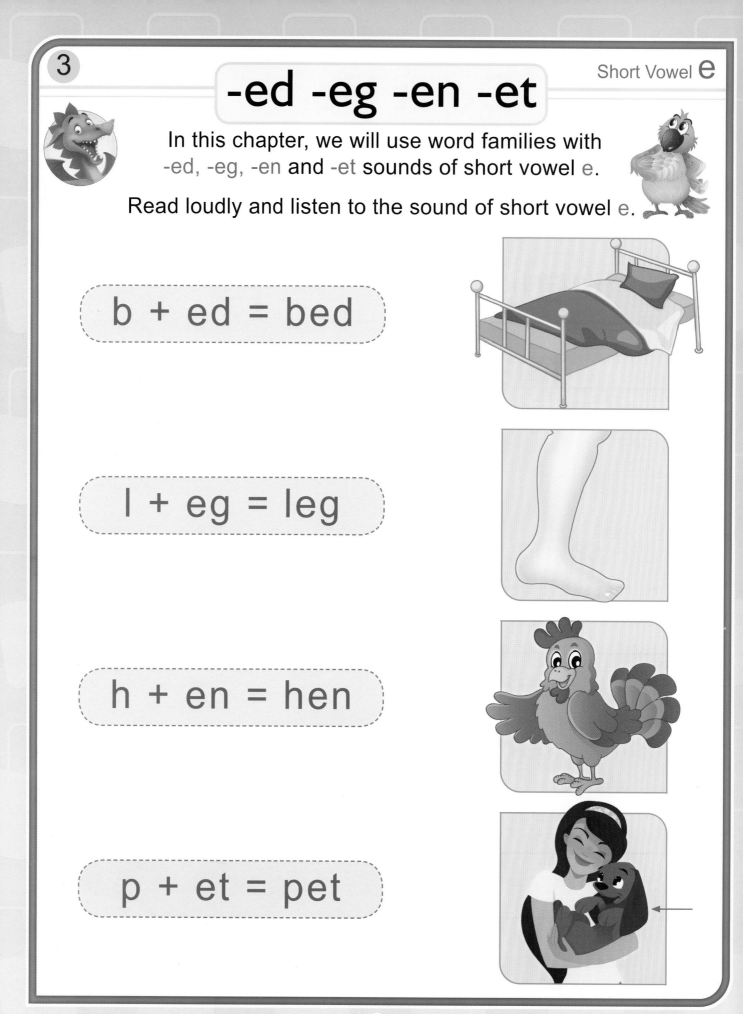

b + ed = bed

l + eg = leg

h + en = hen

p + et = pet

Here are some more new words for you.

-ed

led   fed   red   wed

-eg

Meg   peg   beg   keg

-en

pen   men   ten   den

-et

vet   net   jet   wet

Time to Solve

Join the letters to find the names of the pictures given. One has been done for you.

r b e d
e
d

l
p e g
g

v
p e t
t

m
d e n
n

w
f e d
d

k
b e g
g

Say the names of the pictures and cross the one with sound not matching with its group.

Unscramble the letters to get the correct names of the pictures.

ekg ----------

tve ----------

ent ----------

edf ----------

enh ----------

etp ----------

Read the word and circle the correct picture.

net

keg

pen

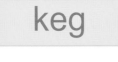

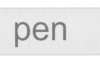

Say the names of the pictures and fill in the missing letters.

p _____

l _____

t _____

r _____

h _____

n _____

See the picture and circle the correct word.

men | ten

vet | net

beg | keg

wed | red

bed | led

den | hen

Look at the pictures and match them to their names.

ten

jet

wed

beg

pen

hen

Time to Chant

My pet hen, laid eggs ten,

Three little boys, chased the poor hen,

The hen ran, ran, ran,

Till she reached the lion's den.

Story Time

Read this story aloud.

Sight Words — a, on, the, an, from

A wet hen on the jet.

The wet hen falls sick.

The vet cures the hen.

The vet gets an egg
from the hen.

Do at Home

Circle the -ed, -eg, -en and -et words and also write them. One has been done for you.

A (vet) with a pet.

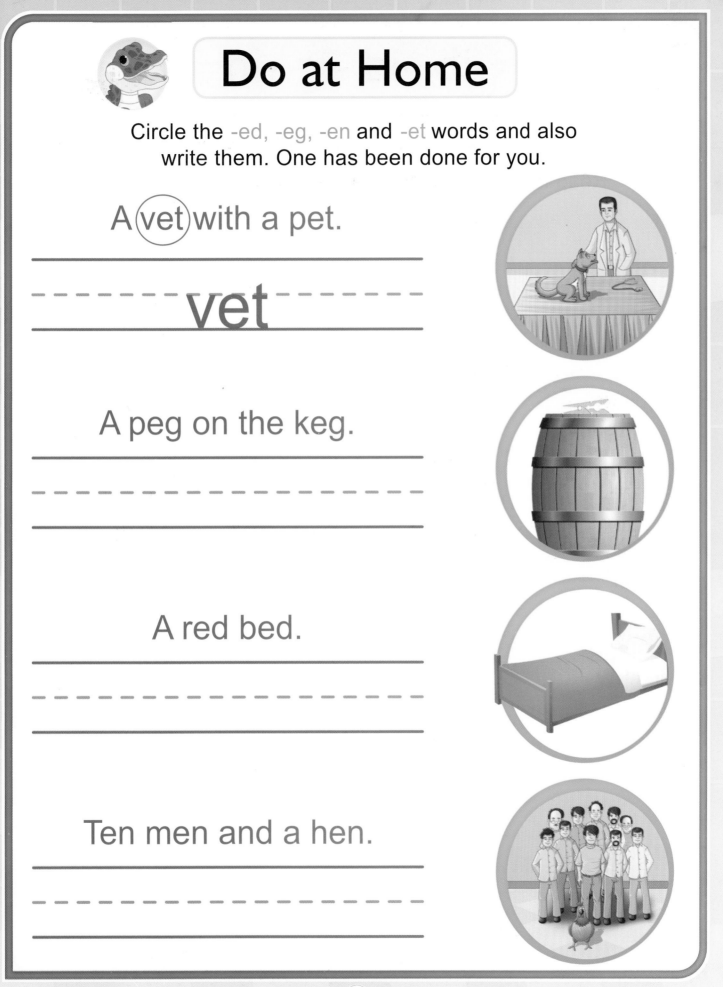

_____

vet

_____

A peg on the keg.

_____

_____

A red bed.

_____

_____

Ten men and a hen.

_____

_____

-ib -id -ig -in

In this chapter, we will use word families with -ib, -id, -ig and -in sounds of short vowel i.

Read loudly and listen to the sound of short vowel i.

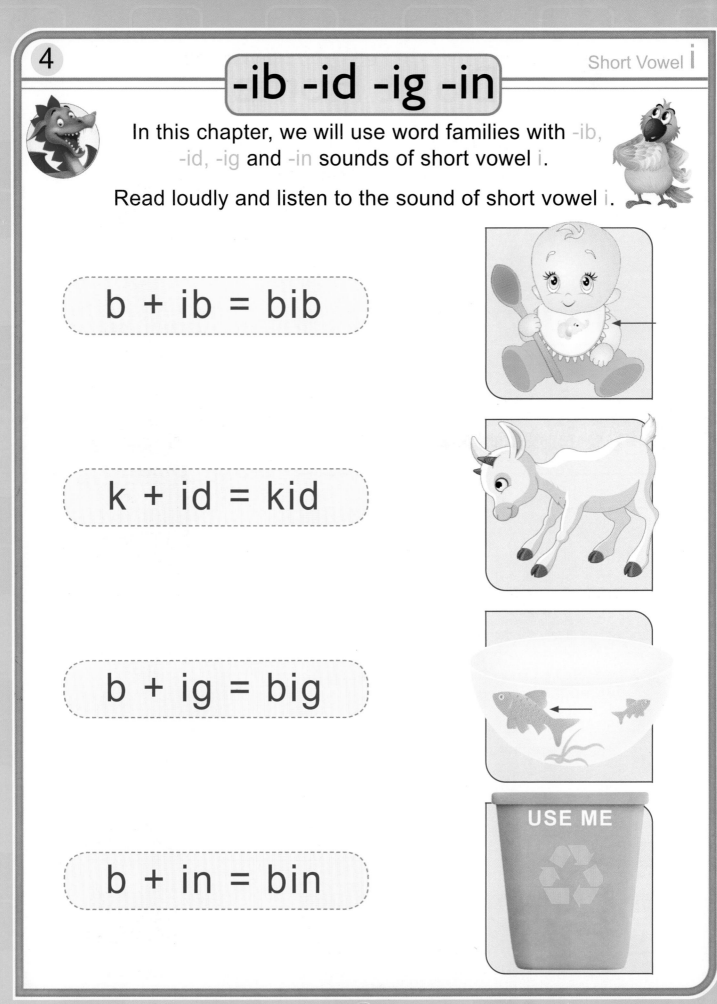

b + ib = bib

k + id = kid

b + ig = big

USE ME

b + in = bin

Here are some more new words for you.

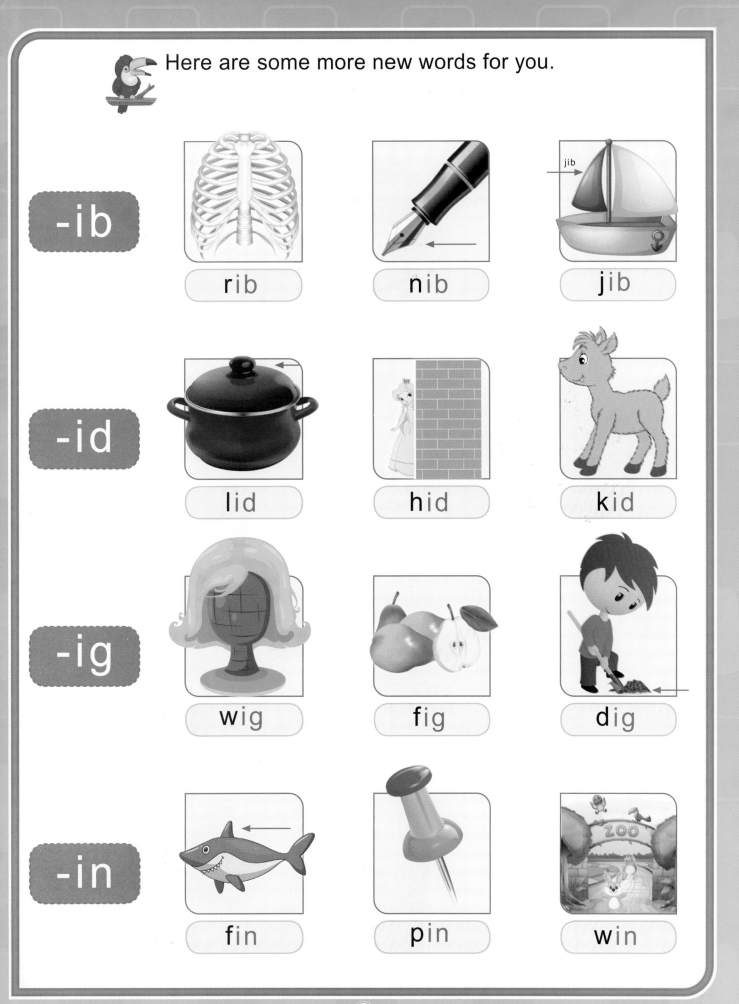

-ib

rib

nib

jib

-id

lid

hid

kid

-ig

wig

fig

dig

-in

fin

pin

win

Circle the two pictures in each row which have the same word sound.

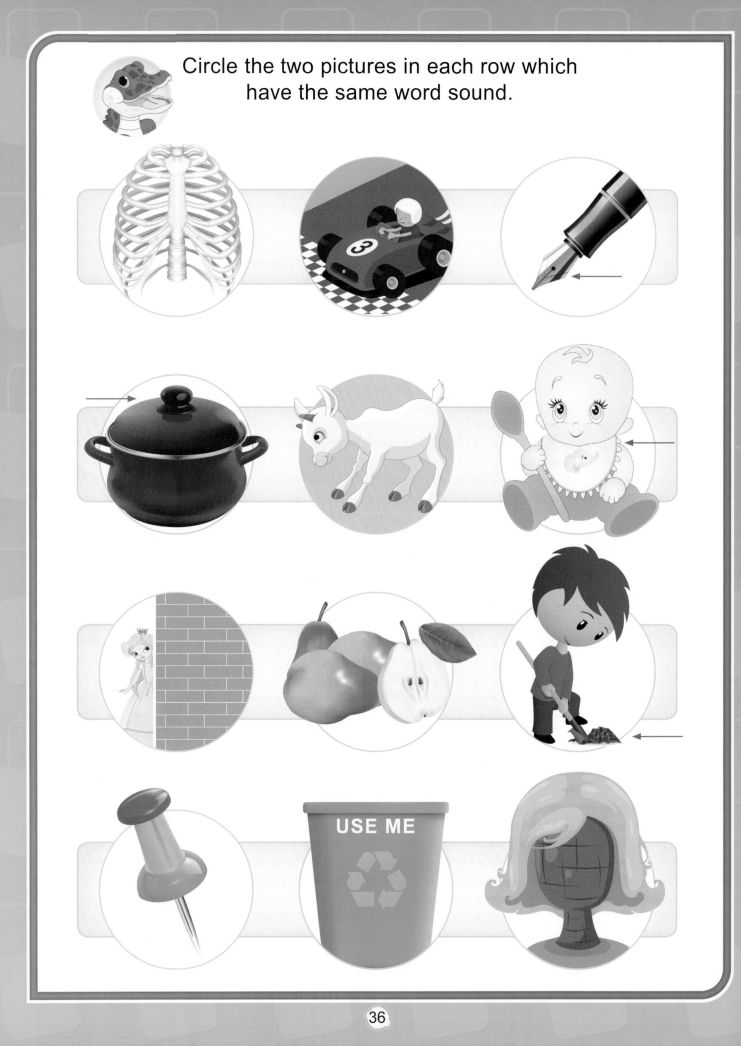

Read the word and circle the correct picture.

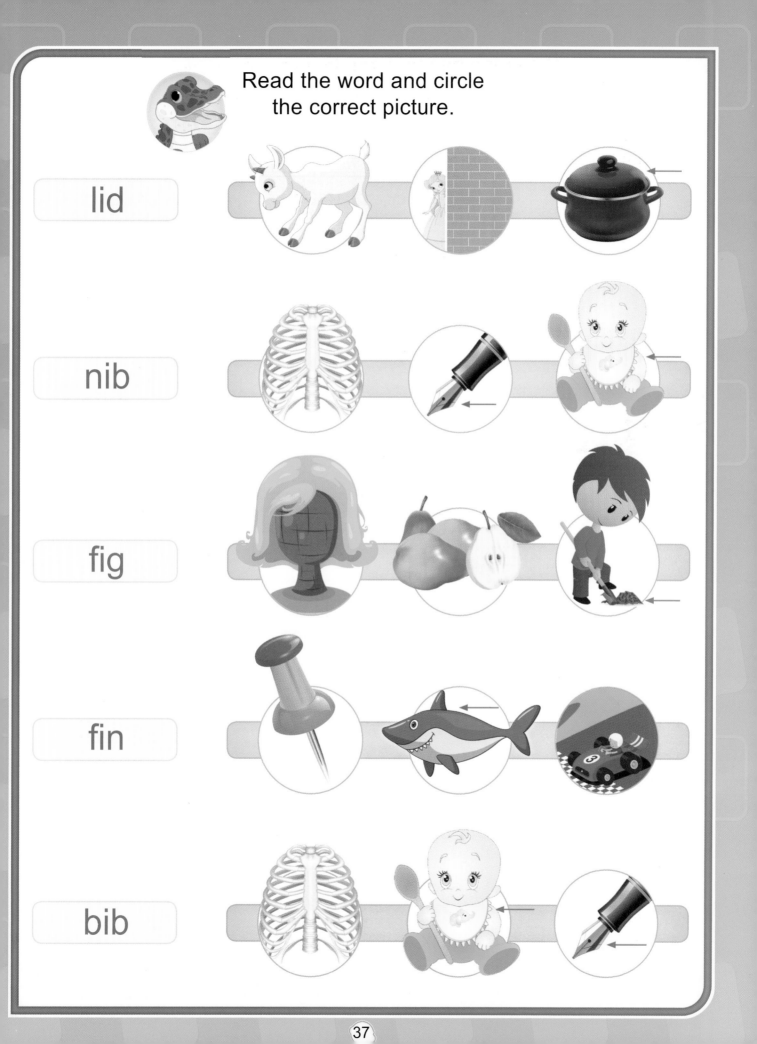

lid

nib

fig

fin

bib

Time to Solve

Unscramble the letters to get the correct names of the pictures.

bbi ------- **inp** ------- **dil** -------

gfi ------- **dik** ------- **nbi** -------

Look at the pictures and circle
their correct names.

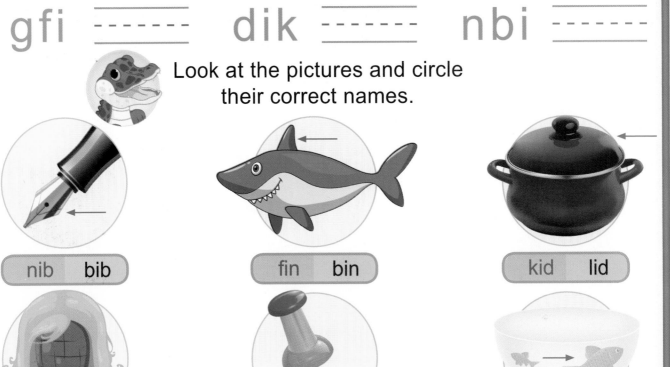

nib   bib   fin   bin   kid   lid

wig   dig   pin   bin   big   fig

Help Peter, the rabbit, reach his burrow
naming the things on his way.

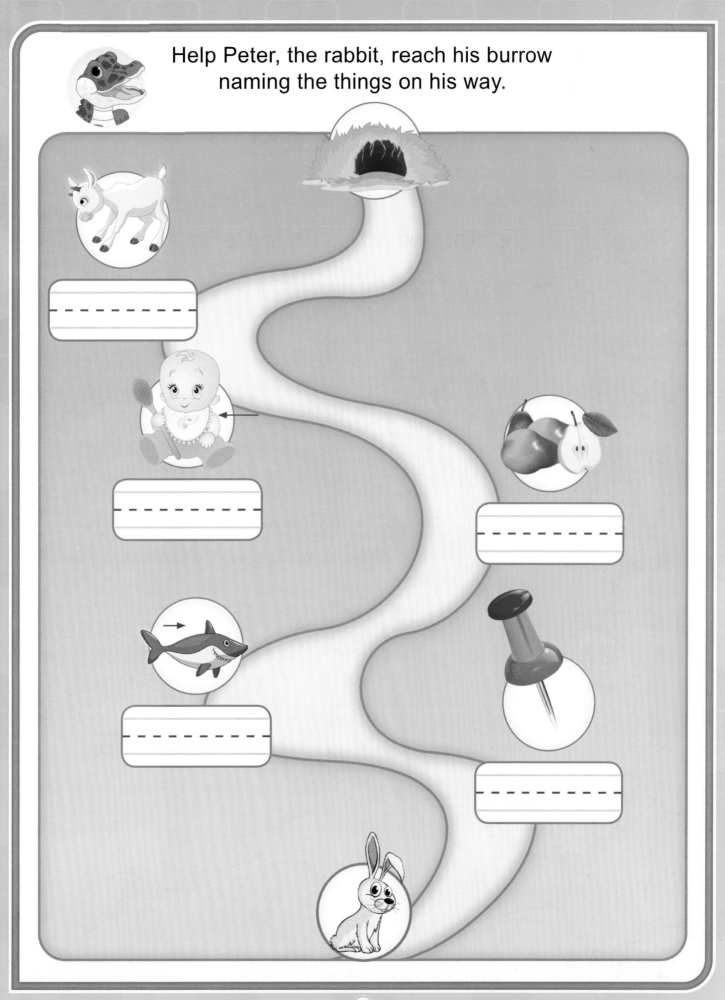

Time to Chant

Three kids near the bin,

One kid jumps into the bin and finds a wig,

The other kid gets a pin and a fig,

The third kid looks at the kid with the fig.

Story Time

Read this story aloud.

The fig is in the bin.

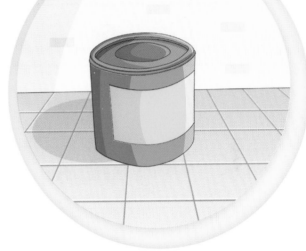

The lid is on the bin.

The kid lifts the lid.

The kid finds the fig and eats it.

Do at Home

Circle the -ib, -id, -ig and -in words and also write them. One has been done for you.

A (pin) on the bin.

_____

pin

_____

Wig and fig.

_____

_____

The nib on a bib.

_____

_____

The kid who hid.

_____

_____

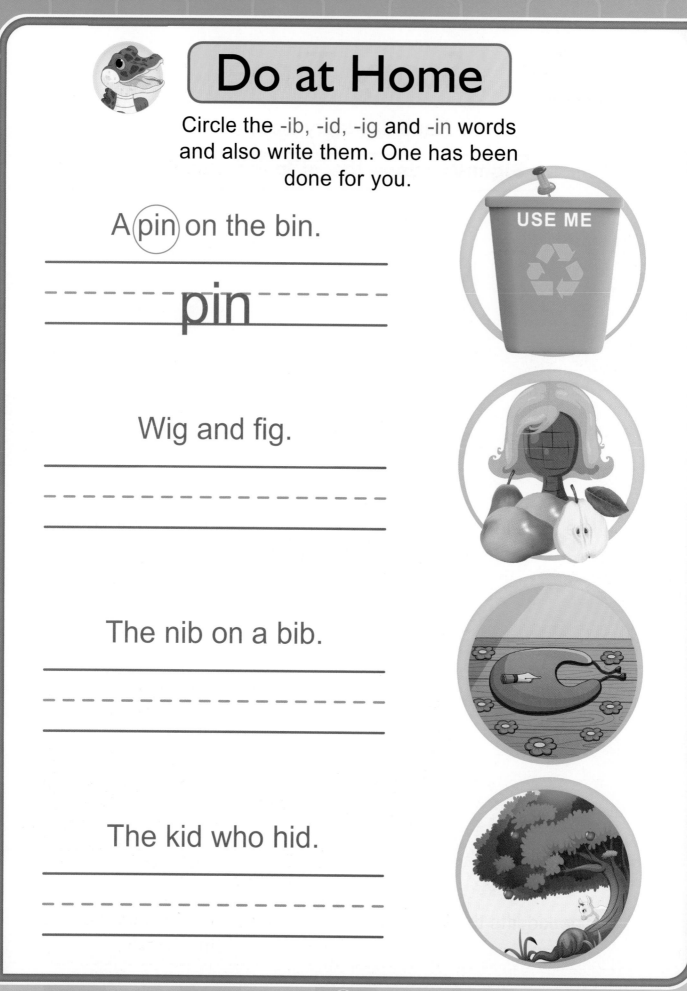

Let Us Revise 1

Short Vowels a, e and i

See the pictures and write their names.

Look at the pictures and write
their names in the boxes.
One has been done for you.

l		
e		
g		

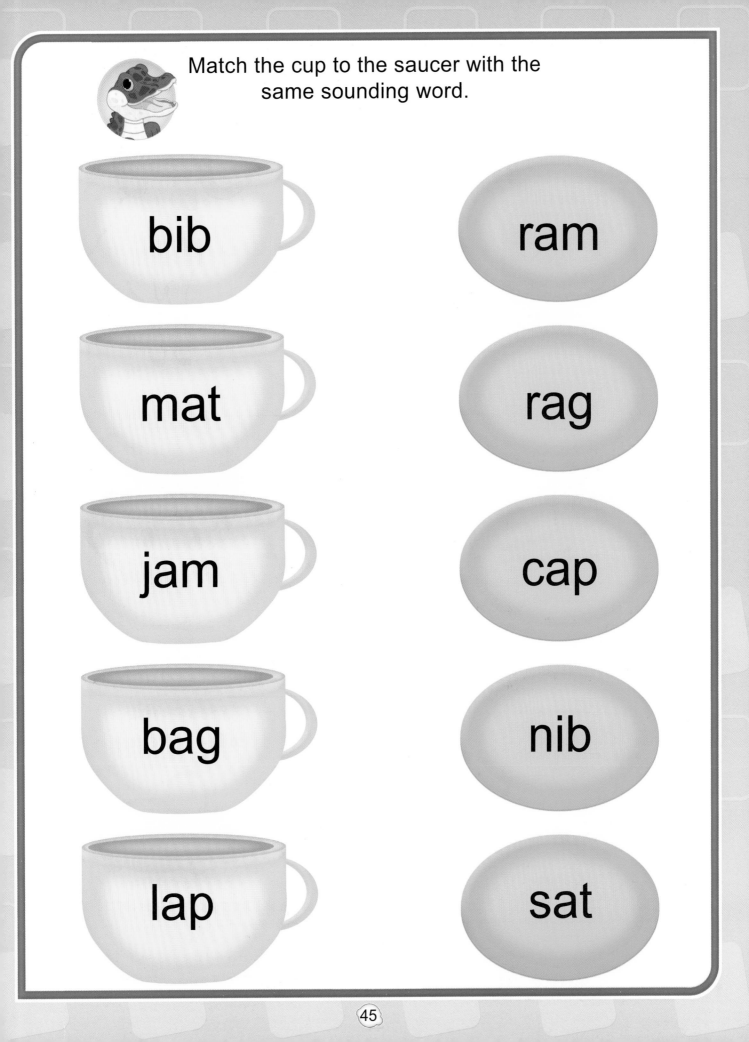

Match the cup to the saucer with the same sounding word.

bib

mat

jam

bag

lap

ram

rag

cap

nib

sat

45

Say the names of the pictures and cross the one with sound not matching with its group.

------- -------

------- -------

------- -------

------- -------

------- -------

------- -------

See the names in the bowl and write them under the correct sounds.

bib   leg   bat

dam   cat   peg

pen   ten   ram

nib

at   am   eg   en   ib

Fill in the blanks and look at
the pictures for clues.

The man in the ....

A .... on the mat

A sad ....

A big ....

Men in the ....

A .... bed

-ip -it -ix

In this chapter, we will use word families with -ip, -it and -ix sounds of short vowel i.

Read loudly and listen to the sound of short vowel i.

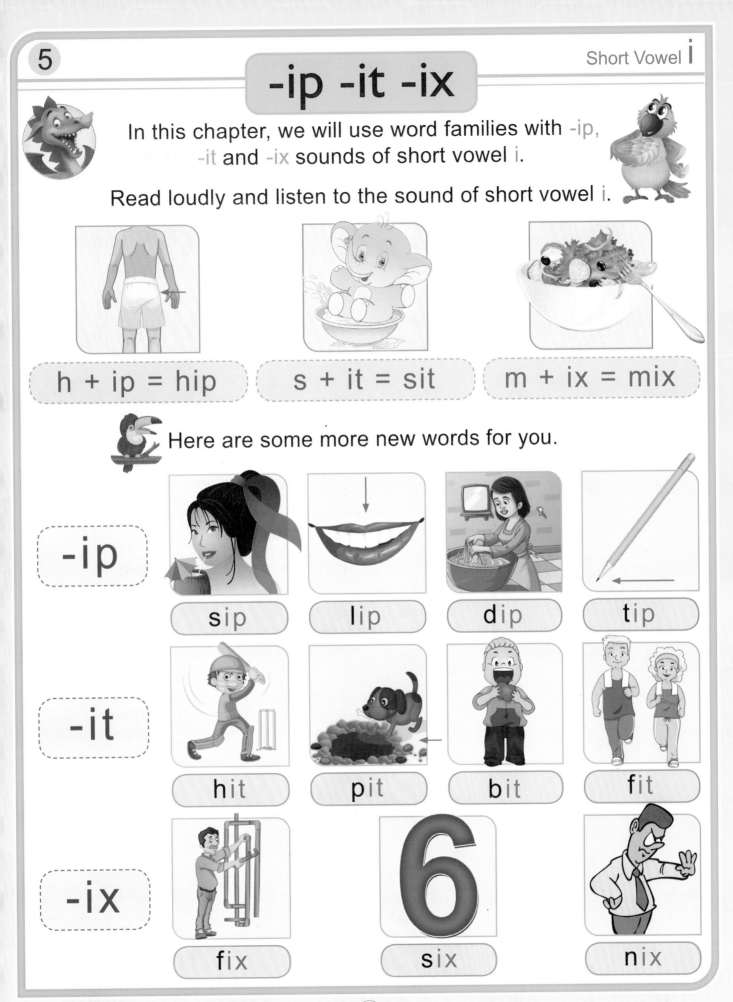

h + ip = hip   s + it = sit   m + ix = mix

Here are some more new words for you.

-ip   sip   lip   dip   tip

-it   hit   pit   bit   fit

-ix   fix   six   nix

Look at the pictures and write their names.

Unscramble the letters to get
the correct names of the pictures.

xim --------

ipt --------

idp --------

ibt --------

pis --------

pil --------

Read the words given on the flower petals and write two more words with the same word sounds.

sit

lip

fix

Look at the pictures and circle their correct names.

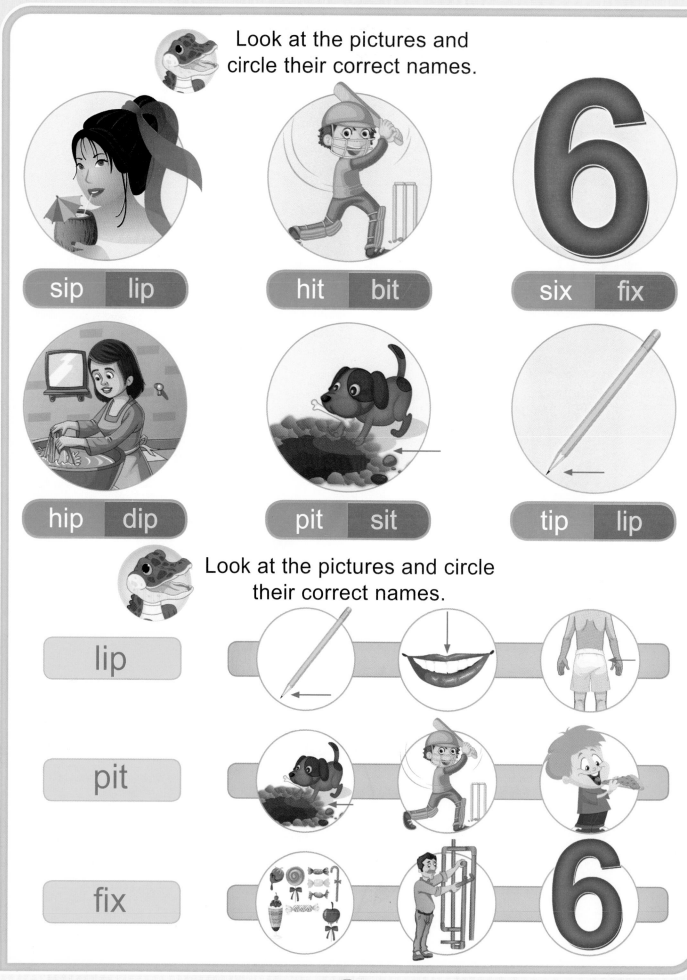

sip | lip

hit | bit

six | fix

hip | dip

pit | sit

tip | lip

Look at the pictures and circle their correct names.

lip

pit

fix

Match the pictures
to their names.

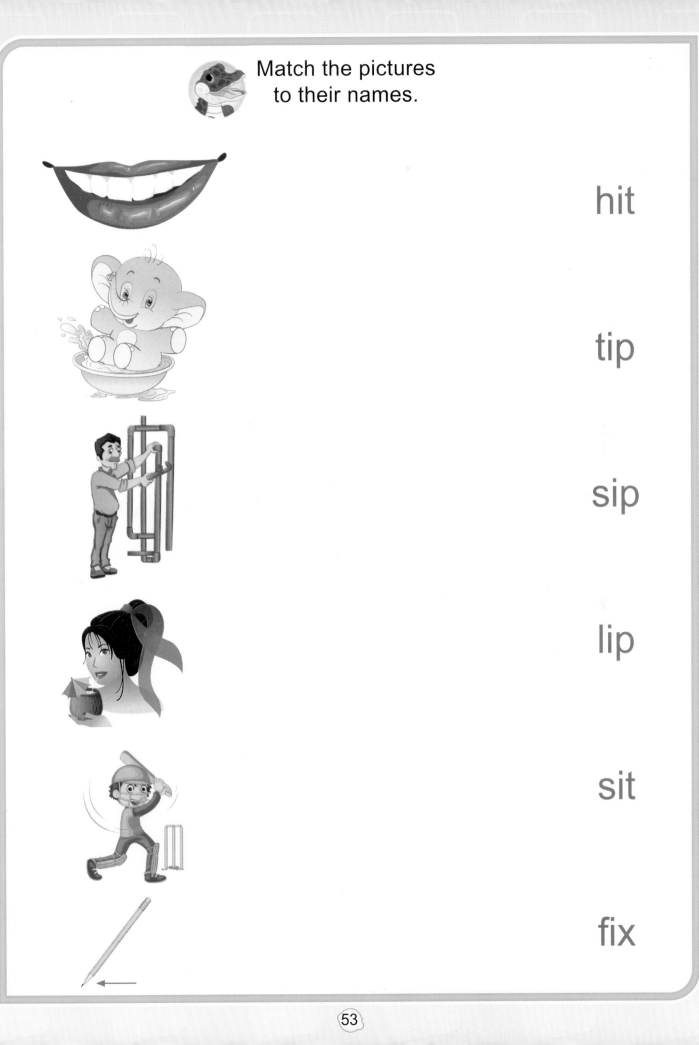

hit

tip

sip

lip

sit

fix

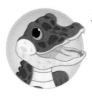

Say the names of the pictures and cross the one with sound not matching with its group.

Time to Chant

Six little cats, sit on the wall,

Six little glasses, six little straws,

Sip! sip! sip! they sip the mix,

Lick! lick! lick! they lick their lips.

Story Time

Read this story aloud.

Ronny sits on the couch.

Six milk shakes for Ronny

Sip, sip, sip!
Ronny sips the shakes.

Ronny licks his lips.

Do at Home

Circle the -ip, -it, and -ix words and also write them. One has been done for you.

(Fix) the mix.

F ix

Sit near the pit.

Tip of the nib.

-og -op -ot -ox

In this chapter, we will use word families with -og, -op, -ot and -ox sounds of short vowel o.

Read loudly and listen to the sound of short vowel o.

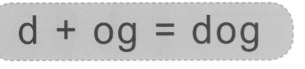
d + og = dog

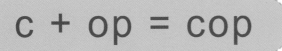
c + op = cop

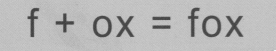
h + ot = hot

f + ox = fox

Here are some more new words for you.

-og

f og   j og   l og   c og

-op

t op   m op   p op   h op

-ot

l ot   p ot   d ot   c ot

-ox

o x   b ox   c ox   p ox

Time to Solve

Look at the pictures and circle their correct names.

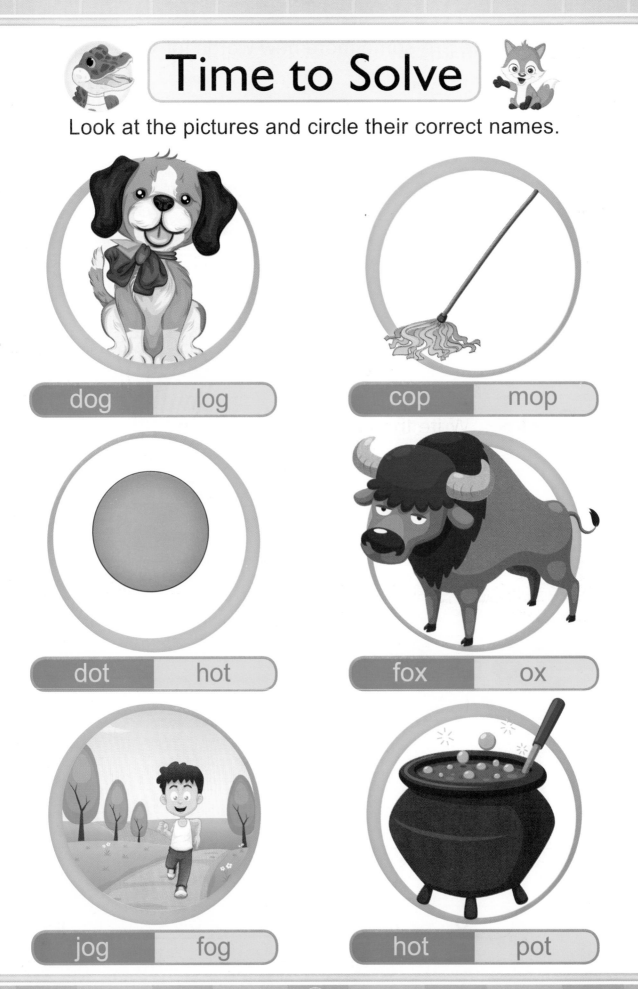

dog	log

cop	mop

dot	hot

fox	ox

jog	fog

hot	pot

Read the name written on each strawberry and write one more name with the same sound.

log

hop

dot

ox

Write the names of the pictures.

See the pictures and
match them to their names.

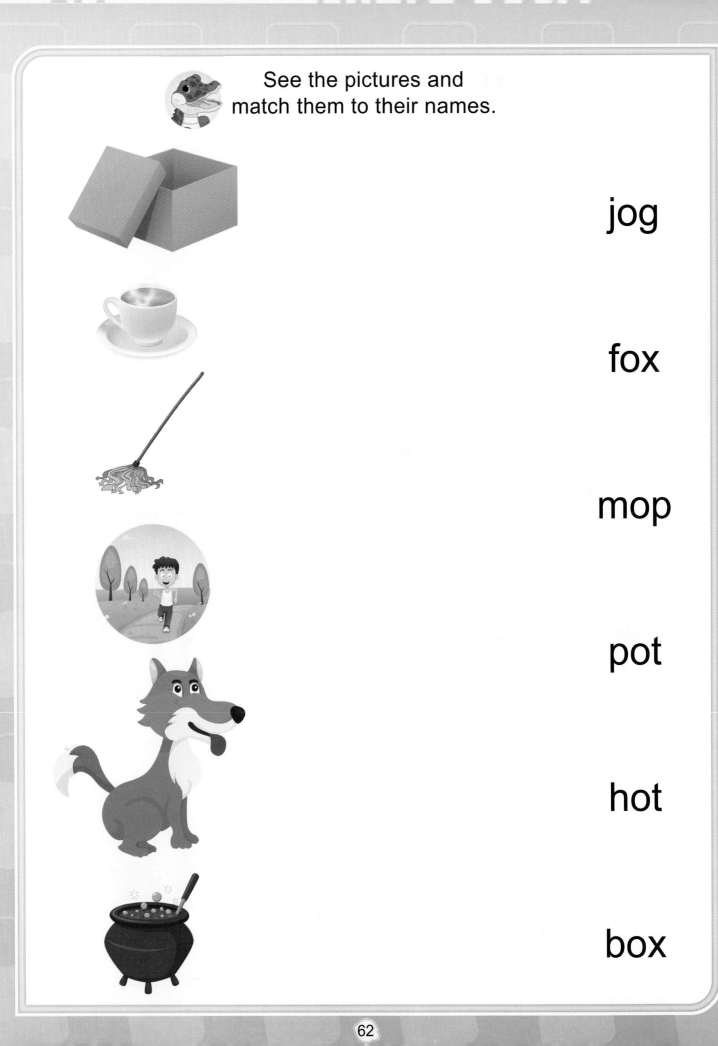

jog

fox

mop

pot

hot

box

Say the names of the pictures and cross the one with sound not matching with its group.

Unscramble the letters to get the correct names of the pictures.

ojg ------

obx ------

pto ------

ppo -------

dgo ------

oth ------

Read the word and circle the correct picture.

fog

cop

dot

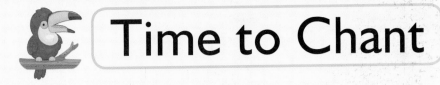

Time to Chant

There is a cat on top of a log,

The cat began to jog, there came a cop;

The cop had a pot, the pot was hot,

He called an ox, but there came a fox;

With a big, big box.

Story Time

Read this story aloud.

Sight Words — a, on, the, is, of, and, an

A dog on the jog

The day is full of fog.

The dog meets a fox
and an ox.

The fox and the ox join
the dog in the jog.

Do at Home

Circle the -og, -op, -ot and -ox words and also write them. One has been done for you.

A (pot) on the cot

pot

A dog on the log

A cop with a mop

A fox with a box

-ub -ug -up

7

In this chapter, we will use word families with -ub, -ug and -up sounds of short vowel u.

Read loudly and listen to the sound of short vowel u.

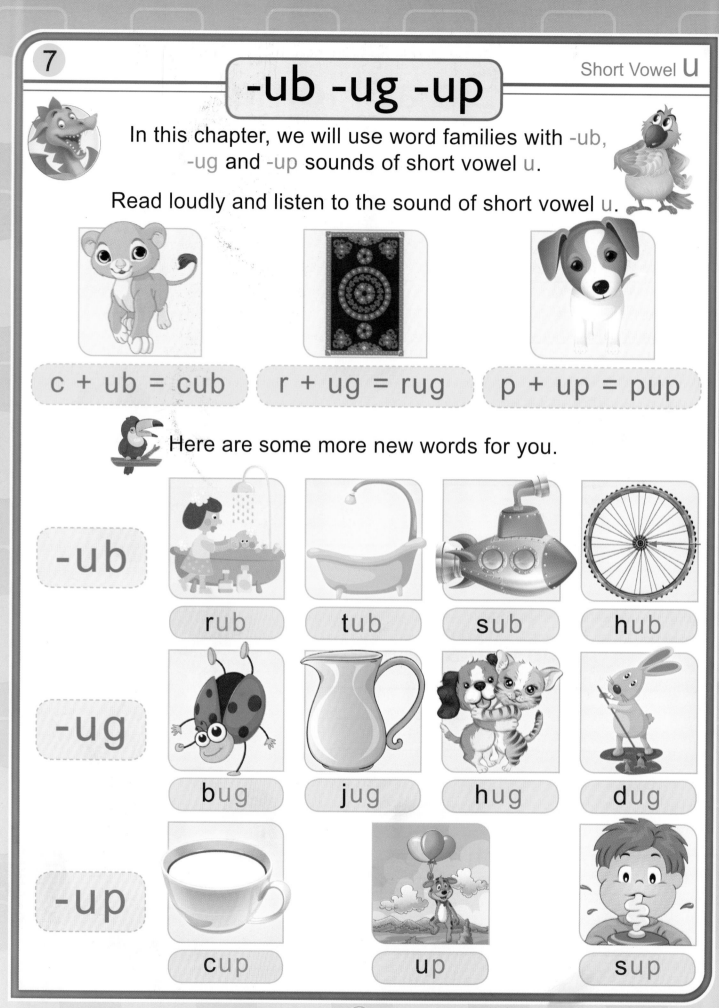

c + ub = cub

r + ug = rug

p + up = pup

Here are some more new words for you.

-ub

rub

tub

sub

hub

-ug

bug

jug

hug

dug

-up

cup

up

sup

Time to Solve

Write the names of the pictures.

- -

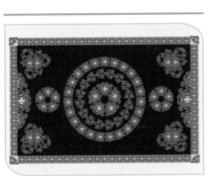  

- -

Read the word and circle the correct picture.

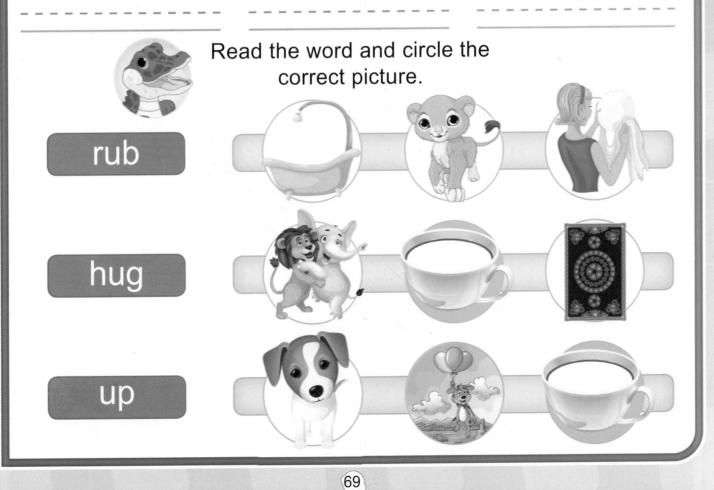

rub

hug

up

Unscramble the letters to get the correct names of the pictures.

bus --------

guh --------

ppu --------

but --------

gbu --------

puc --------

Look at the pictures and circle their correct names.

cub   rub

hug   jug

pup   cup

tub   sub

up   cup

rug   hug

Find the words in the boxes and write them.
You can look at the pictures for clues.

| t | a | c | u | b | z |

_____

- - - - - - - - - - - -

_____

| s | b | g | b | u | g |

_____

- - - - - - - - - - - -

_____

| p | u | p | g | h | x |

_____

- - - - - - - - - - - -

_____

| i | e | s | u | b | x |

_____

- - - - - - - - - - - -

_____

Find out the words given in the crossword.
You can look at the pictures for clues.

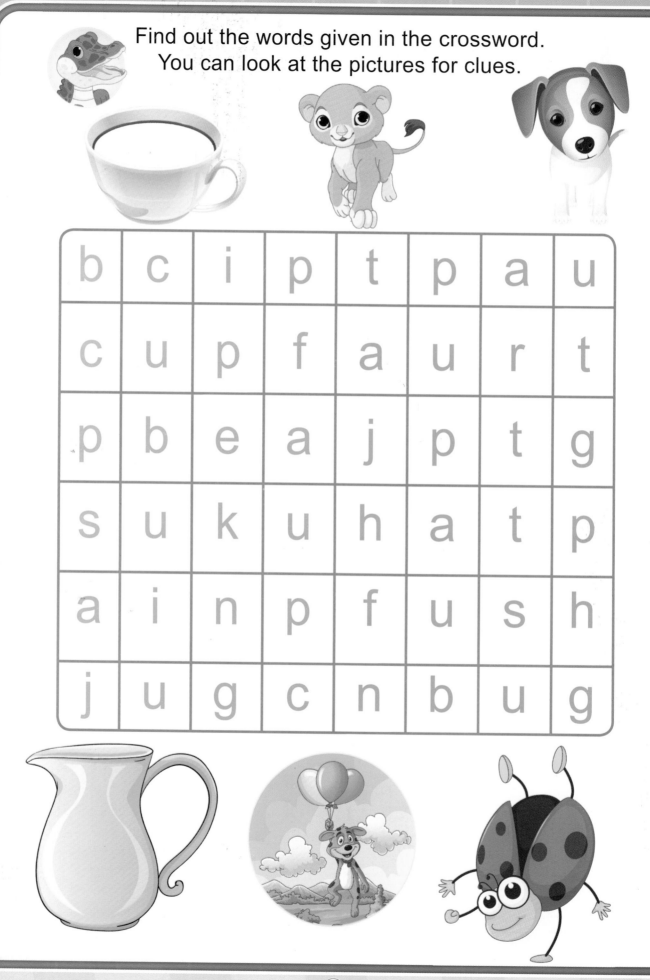

b	c	i	p	t	p	a	u
c	u	p	f	a	u	r	t
p	b	e	a	j	p	t	g
s	u	k	u	h	a	t	p
a	i	n	p	f	u	s	h
j	u	g	c	n	b	u	g

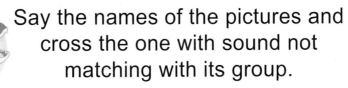 Say the names of the pictures and cross the one with sound not matching with its group.

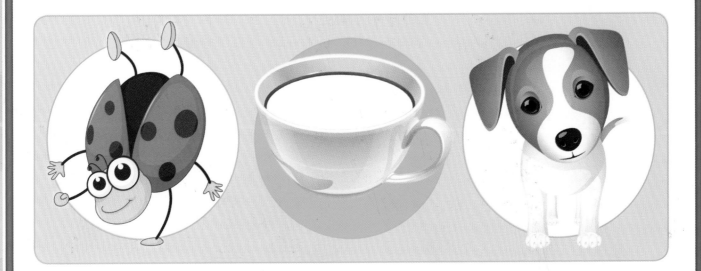

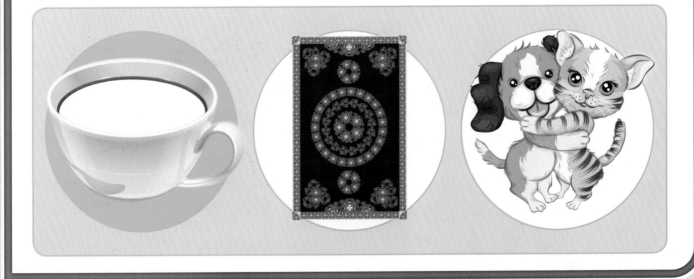

Time to Chant

A pup and a bug, stand on a rug,

They watch a cub, sitting in a tub,

Dreaming of a sub,

The tiger asks the dog, "What's up?"

They give each other a close hug.

Story Time

Read this story aloud.

Sight Words — the, is, in, on

The pup is in
the tub.

The pup is wet.

The cub rubs
the pup.

The cub puts the pup
on the rug.

Do at Home

Circle the -ub, -ug and -up words and also write them.
One has been done for you.

A (bug) on the rug

bug

A cub in the sub

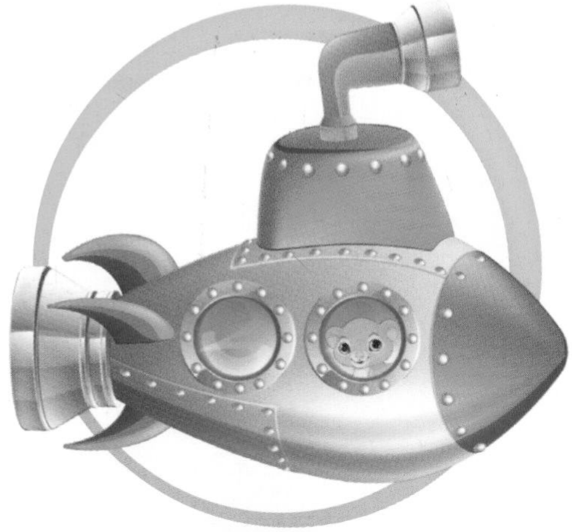

A pup going up

-ud -un -ut

In this chapter, we will use word families with -ud, -un and -ut sounds of short vowel u.

Read loudly and listen to the sound of short vowel u.

b + ud = bud

r + un = run

n + ut = nut

Here are some more new words for you.

-ud

mud

stud

thud

-un

bun

sun

fun

-ut

cut

hut

gut

Time to Solve

Write the names of the pictures.

Look at the pictures and circle
their correct names.

bun   sun

mud   bud

nut   cut

fun   bun

cut   hut

sun   run

Unscramble the letters to get the correct names of the pictures.

snu ------   dum ------   ctu ------

ntu ------   bdu ------   bnu ------

Join the letters to find the names of the pictures given. One has been done for you.

b
m u d
d

b
s u n
n

c
h u t
t

f
r u n
n

79

Find the words in the boxes and write them.
You can look at the pictures for clues.

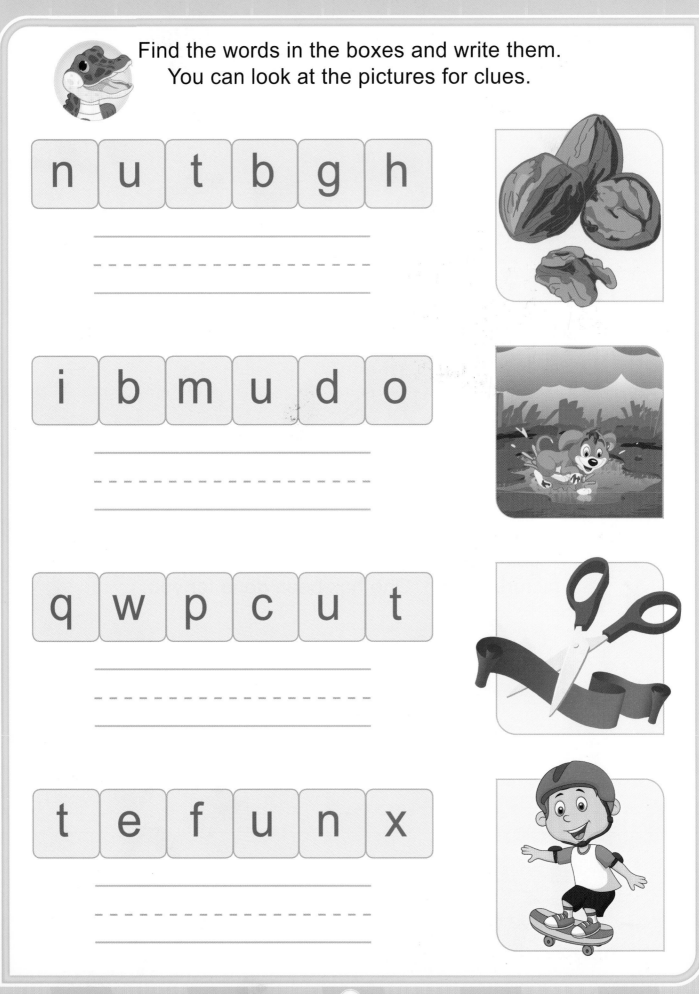

n u t b g h

i b m u d o

q w p c u t

t e f u n x

See the pictures and
match them to their names.

mud

sun

bun

cut

nut

bud

Write the names of the pictures and cross the one with sound not matching with its group.

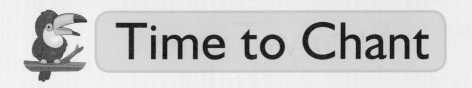

Time to Chant

Near the hut, under the sun,

Children have fun, eating nuts and buns;

They run, run, run.

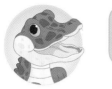

Story Time

Read this story aloud.

Sight Words — this, is, a, in, the, on

This is Bunny's hut.

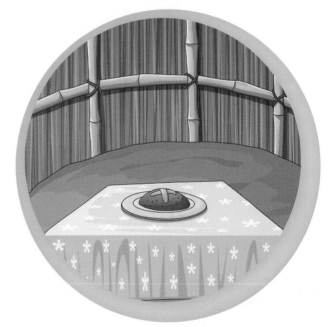

Bunny has a bun in the hut.

Bunny gets the bun.

Bunny puts a nut on the bun.

Circle the -ud, -un and -ut words and also write them. One has been done for you.

It is (fun) to run.

fun

A nut near the hut

A rose bud with some mud

Let Us Revise 2

Short Vowels i, o, and u

See the pictures and write their names.

Look at the pictures and tick the correct name from the options given.

cub   sub   cop

cut   pit   cup

bun   hut   rug

bud   pot   run

fix   hot   nut

fox   hop   cut

Look at the pictures and write their names in the boxes. One has been done for you.

| s | u | b |

Match the pictures with the same
sounding words.

Complete the words with correct endings.

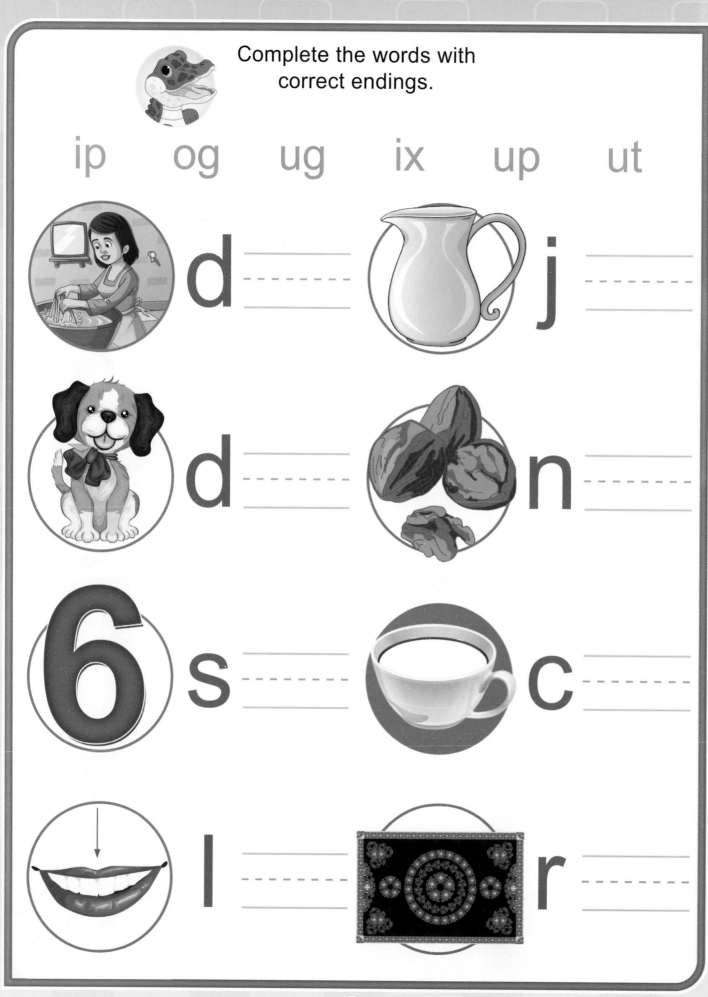

ip   og   ug   ix   up   ut

d _____   j _____

d _____   n _____

s _____   c _____

l _____   r _____

Fill in the blanks and look at the pictures for clues.

Zip your ....

A .... in the box

A .... in the tub

A .... on the rug

A hot ....

A .... on the log

Let's Review

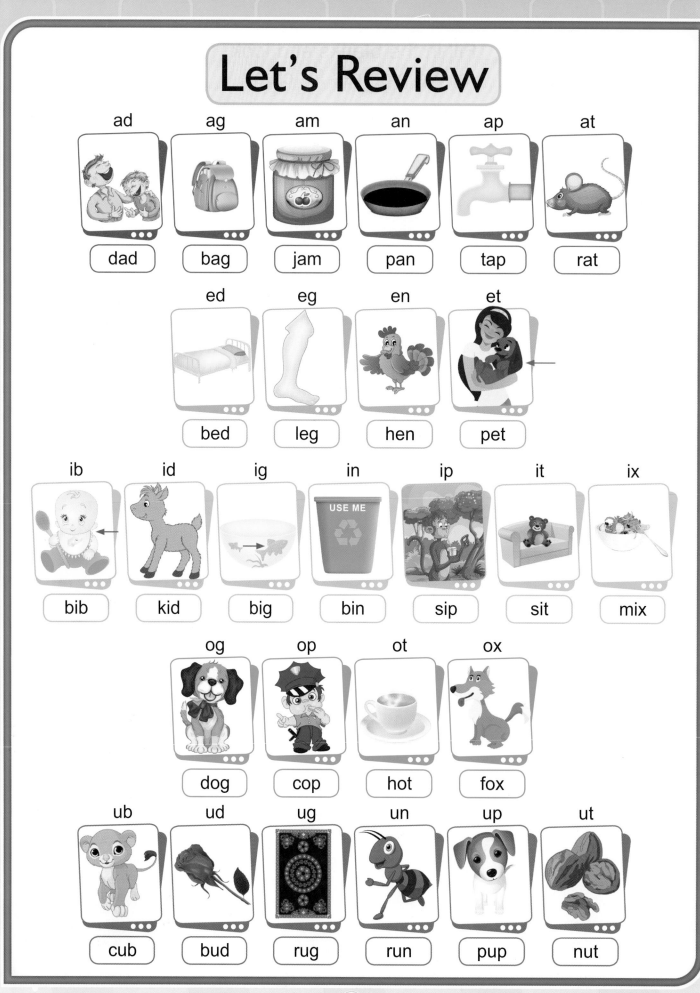

ad	ag	am	an	ap	at
dad	bag	jam	pan	tap	rat

ed	eg	en	et
bed	leg	hen	pet

ib	id	ig	in	ip	it	ix
bib	kid	big	bin	sip	sit	mix

og	op	ot	ox
dog	cop	hot	fox

ub	ud	ug	un	up	ut
cub	bud	rug	run	pup	nut

Write the appropriate word in the same word sound box.

yam, net, mat, dig, pen, rib, keg, cap, tag, can, pin, sip, hid, sad, red, hit, six, log, mop, cot, box, tub, up, bug, mud, hut, sun

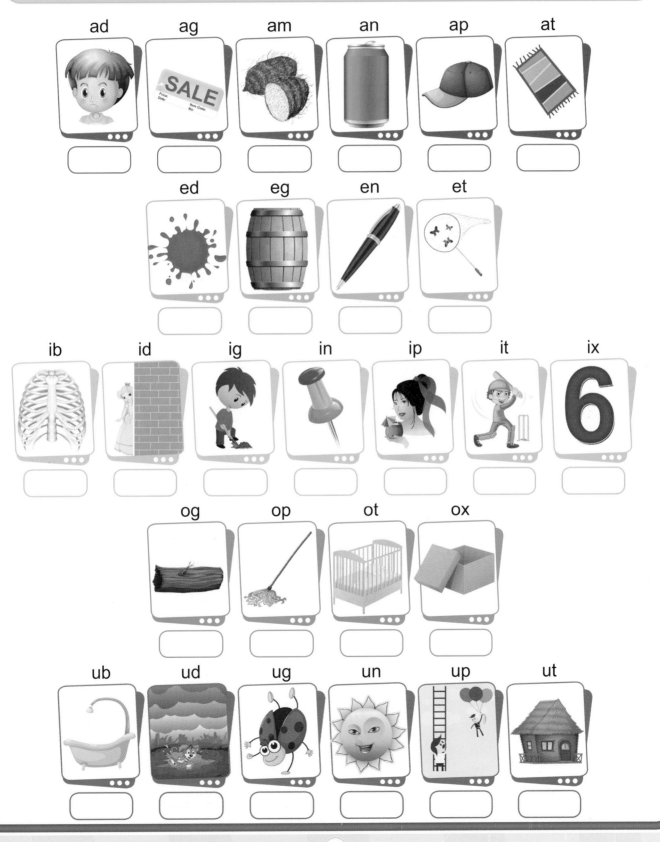

ad   ag   am   an   ap   at

ed   eg   en   et

ib   id   ig   in   ip   it   ix

og   op   ot   ox

ub   ud   ug   un   up   ut

Picture Reading

Look at the collage and read the names of the items given below in the collage. Circle the items that you can spot in the collage.

hut	bed	jug	sun	lid
kid	keg	top	hug	sip
bin	fig	box	nut	
ten	hip	cub	stud	
mat	cop	map	men	

Picture Recognition

The pictures given below have vowel sounds in their names.
Look at the pictures and write their names.

Picture Recognition

Read the words under each picture and circle the correct word.

| bat | but | bit |

| pan | pin | pen |

| pat | pit | pot |

| nit | net | nut |

| log | leg | lag |

| bat | bet | bin |

| fox | fax | fix |

| big | bug | bag |

| cat | cot | cut |

| rug | rig | rag |

| pig | pug | peg |

| fin | fan | fun |